How to play
TABLE
TENNIS

a step·by·step guide

Series editor:
Mike Shaw

Technical consultant: Ken Edwards,
General Secretary, Norwich and
District Table Tennis League

JARROLD

Other titles in this series are:

How to play TENNIS
SQUASH
BADMINTON
CROQUET
BOWLS

How to play TABLE TENNIS
ISBN 0-7117-0425-2
First published in Great Britain, 1989
Copyright © Mike Shaw, 1989

Designed and produced by
Parke Sutton Limited, 8 Thorpe Road,
Norwich NR1 1RY
for Jarrold Colour Publications, Barrack Street,
Norwich NR3 1TR
Illustrations by Malcolm Ryan

Printed in Portugal

Contents

Introduction

Most people have played table tennis at some time or other. Because it is played indoors, requires little equipment and is freely available in sports halls, social clubs and youth centres, it is an ideal recreation to adopt.

Although it takes its name and many of its rules from lawn tennis, the comparison ends there. Table tennis is quite unlike any other sport. The lightness of the ball and the small area of the table make it a game of great delicacy requiring lightning reflexes, great agility and, if played to a reasonable standard, a high level of physical fitness.

Because most people are familiar with the game, there is a tendency to take it lightly. This is a mistake if you have any desire at all to play well. There is much more to the game than playing 'ping pong' would suggest.

It is important to be aware from the outset of the various strokes and spin techniques. Even though you may not be able to master them initially, your early play should be a preparation for their gradual introduction.

By far the best way to start is with a qualified coach. These operate throughout the country and can be contacted via the English Table Tennis Association at Queensbury House, Havelock Road, Hastings, East Sussex TN34 1HF. It is very difficult to 'unlearn' bad technique and coaching will get you off to an excellent − and enjoyable − start.

The Table

Table tennis was traditionally played on thick wooden tables, but today there are also composite wood, slate, glass, plastic and even metal varieties which are just as satisfactory.

The essential property for a table, apart from being level and flat, is that at any point a regulation ball will bounce between 22cm and 25cm when dropped from a height of 30.5cm (see diagram below).

The surface of the table should have a matt finish and is usually dark green, blue or grey. In time this becomes shiny and reflective and requires resurfacing.

Lighting is extremely important. Tungsten halogen lamps are ideal. It is essential that the entire playing area rather than just the table is well lit.

The playing area should be a minimum of 8.83m long and 4.57m wide.

The nature of the floor is also of extreme importance. Certain flooring, because of its elasticity, can affect the bounce of the ball on the table. Light-coloured flooring makes seeing the ball difficult; slippery flooring makes playing difficult.

If possible, the background walls too, should be dark-coloured and non-reflective.

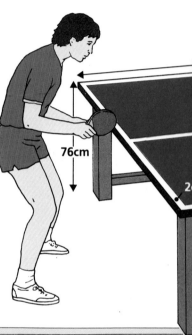

76cm

The bounce

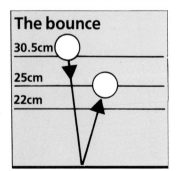

30.5cm

25cm

22cm

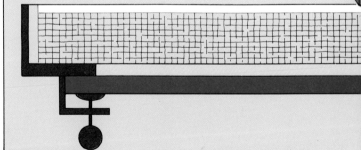

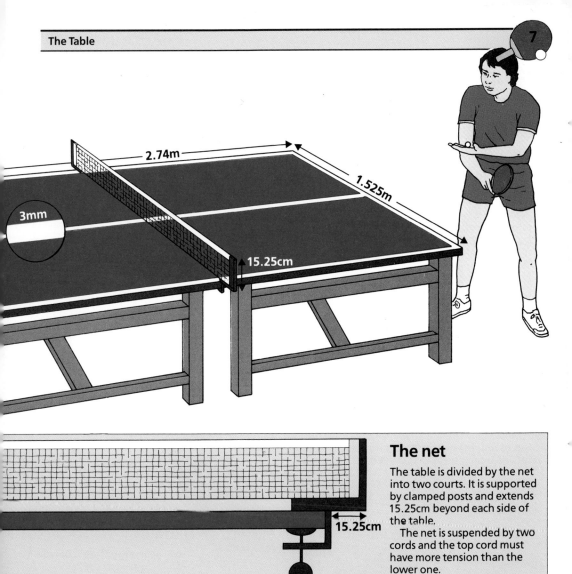

2.74m

1.525m

3mm

15.25cm

The net

The table is divided by the net into two courts. It is supported by clamped posts and extends 15.25cm beyond each side of the table.

15.25cm

The net is suspended by two cords and the top cord must have more tension than the lower one.

Equipment

The basic equipment required is a bat and a ball.

Table tennis bats

A table tennis bat may be of any size, shape or weight.

Beginners should start with a five-ply bat. This is the number of layers of wood (or other materials) which make up the blade. There can be as few as one or as many as seven. Blade shapes vary between square, oval or nearly round. Shape is very much a matter of choice.

The blade is covered with a further layer of rubber, or sponge rubber and rubber. The rubber may be smooth or with evenly distributed 'pimples' (between 10 and 50 pimples to the half inch). The pimples can face outwards, or inwards onto the sponge rubber (known as 'reversed rubber').

If covered with rubber alone, the thickness of either side should not exceed 2mm. If a sponge and rubber sandwich, it should be no thicker than 4mm. Beginners should start with 1.5mm rubber.

The rubbers must be red on one side and black on the other to highlight any difference in the coverings.

Try playing with all the various sizes, weights and compositions before buying an expensive bat. Above all your bat should feel comfortable.

Bats will usually need recovering once or twice a year.

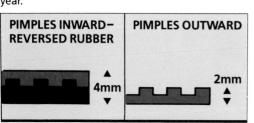

PIMPLES INWARD– REVERSED RUBBER	PIMPLES OUTWARD
▲ 4mm ▼	2mm ▲ ▼

Handles

There are many different handle shapes. The rule is simple, however: play with what feels comfortable.

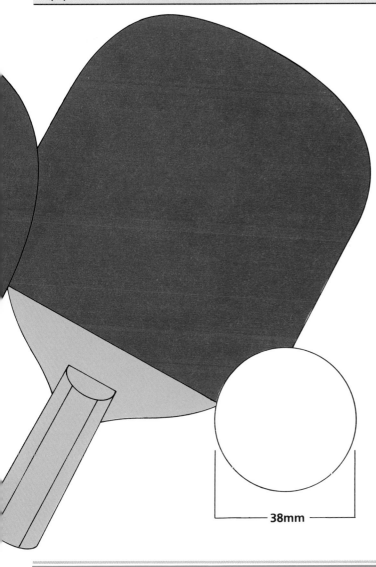

38mm

Table tennis balls

Table tennis balls are made of matt celluloid (or a similar plastic material). They have a diameter of 38mm, weigh 2.5gms and are usually white, but yellow is permitted.

Use good quality (3 star) balls approved by the National Table Tennis Association or International Table Tennis Federation.

Cracked balls

During play balls will crack regularly and have to be thrown away.

There are two ways to test for a cracked ball:

1 Roll the ball gently on the table – if it creaks it is cracked.

2 Spin a ball to test for any irregularity. A true ball will stay on the spot without wobbling in its spin.

Clothing

Table tennis is a fast-moving game involving stretching and running. Clothing should allow freedom of move - ment and footwear should be flexible and supportive.

Clothing can be of any uniform, over-all colour but most not be white. This is because of the difficulty of seeing a fast-moving small white ball. The fewer distractions and changes in background the better.

A track suit is a useful item for keeping warm before and after games, as is a spare shirt for those who perspire a lot.

The Toss

A game begins with the toss of a coin. This is to decide who will serve first and from which end the players will start.

The winner of the toss can either decide who starts serving or choose ends, but not both. Alternatively, the winner of the toss can decide to make his/her opponent make the first choice.

If you win the toss there are four possible outcomes.

1	Choose to serve.	**Opponent chooses ends.**
2	Choose not to serve.	**Opponent serves and chooses end.**
3	Choose ends.	**Opponent chooses who serves.**
4	Choose not to choose.	**Opponent chooses 1, 2, or 3.**

Scoring

In table tennis both the server and the receiver can score a point. So if the server fails to make a good service, for example, the opponent scores a point.

A game is won by the first player or pair to score 21 points, unless the score reaches 20 – 20 in which case play continues until one player or pair has two clear points more than the other. This can be 28 – 26, 23 – 21, or whatever.

A match (between two players or pairs) consists of the best of three games or, occasionally, the best of five games.

The Expedite System

This system is introduced to put a reasonable time limit on games. It comes into operation if a game is unfinished after fifteen minutes (or earlier at the request of both players or pairs).

When the time limit is reached the game stops, whatever the state of play.

1	**If a rally was in progress the server serves the point again.**
2	**If no rally was in progress the previous receiver serves the point.**
3	**Each player serves one point in turn from now on.**
4	**In any point, if the receiver (or receiving pair) makes thirteen good returns they win the point.**
5	**The Expedite System, once introduced, remains in operation for the rest of the match.**

Order of Serving

Singles

One player begins and serves for the first five points.

The service then passes to the opponent who also serves for five points. This continues until one player wins the game (by scoring 21 points) or both players reach a score of twenty points – a deuce situation. In this situation the players alternately serve one point each until the end of the game.

Players change ends after each game, and after ten points in the final deciding game.

The player who served first in the previous game receives first in the next.

Doubles return sequence

In doubles the ball is returned in a strict sequence.

The server serves and the receiver returns. Then the server's partner returns and the receiver's partner returns. This sequence then starts again with the server returning and so on until the end of the point.

Doubles

In doubles the rules of serving and changing ends are the same as in singles, except that the table is divided into two and the service is made from and to the right hand side only. The centre line forms part of the service court.

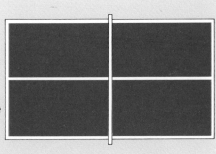

At the beginning of the match the pair to serve choose who will serve first, and, in this first game only, the pair to receive decide who will receive first.

If Team 1 (A & B) is playing Team 2 (C & D) and A is to serve first and C to receive first, the sequence would be as follows:

1 **A serves five times from the right to C.**
2 **The receiver always serves next, so C serves five times from the right to B.**
3 **B serves five times from the right to D.**
4 **D serves five times from the right to A.**
5 **A serves five times from the right to C; and so on.**
 You will note that A always serves to C, C to B, etc. This continues until one side wins or the score reaches 20 – 20, in which case the sequence is the same but the server changes after each service.

The teams change ends and serving sequence after each game (or after 10 points in a decider). The pair who received first in the previous game now serve first.

So as C received first in the previous game, C & D now serve first in the second. They decide D shall serve first. In the previous game B was serving to D so now D serves to B.

By this means any advantages are evened out.

The Service

Each point begins with a service. The server holds the ball stationary in the palm of the free hand, and then tosses it up in the air. Once it has passed its highest point the ball is struck by the bat so that it bounces first on the server's side of the table, clears the net (either over or round) and then bounces on the opponent's side. Anywhere on the top surface of the table, including the line, is in. On the side of the table is out. (See Non-Fault No. 7, page 21.)

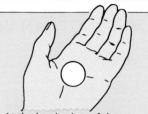

At the beginning of the service the ball must be resting on the free hand (the hand not holding the bat) which should be stationary, open and flat with the fingers together and the thumb free.

The free hand must be above the level of the table.

The whole of the bat must be above the level of the table throughout the service.

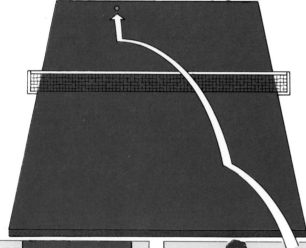

When the ball is struck it must be behind the edge of the table (or an imaginary line extending from it) but not further from the table than the server.

After the ball has passed the highest point of its trajectory it is struck by the bat so that it bounces on the server's side of the table, clears the net and then bounces on the receiver's side.

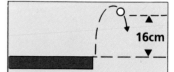

16cm

The ball must be tossed a minimum of 16 cms into the air without any spin.

A return

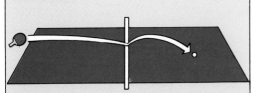

A good return is a single hit of the ball with the bat, or the bat hand below the wrist, after it has bounced on the player's side of the table, so that the ball returns directly onto the opponent's side of the table.

The ball is permitted to hit the net (or the net assembly) on the way.

In doubles there is a sequence for returning the ball. (See Doubles Sequence on page 13.)

A let

If during service the ball hits the net and lands in the receiver's half of the table it is not a fault but the service is taken again. This is called a 'let'. It does not count as a service or as a point. If, however, the ball hits the net and does not land on the receiver's side of the table, or is not a good service for any other reason, it is a fault, and a point to the receiver. If a net service is volleyed (usually inadvertently), a let is played.

A Point

The ball must bounce only once on your side of the table before being hit back to your opponent. This continues until you or your opponent lose the point.

You lose a point if:

1 You fail to make a good service.

2

You return the ball and it hits anything other than your opponent's side of the table, excepting that it may touch the net or net assembly on the way.

3 You fail to return the ball.

4

You volley the ball (i.e. hit it before it has bounced on your side of the table).

5

The ball bounces twice on your side of the table.

Service Faults

Making any of these faults while serving loses the point.

1 Hand below table level

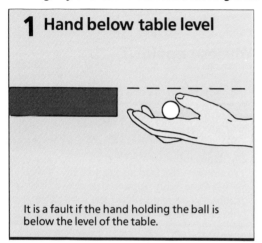

It is a fault if the hand holding the ball is below the level of the table.

2 Bat below table level

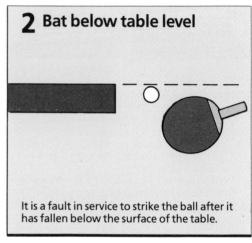

It is a fault in service to strike the ball after it has fallen below the surface of the table.

3 Ball over the table

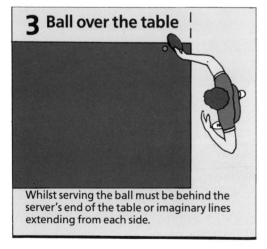

Whilst serving the ball must be behind the server's end of the table or imaginary lines extending from each side.

4 Ball behind the server

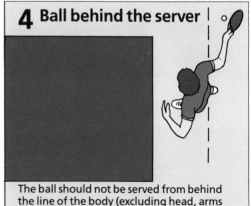

The ball should not be served from behind the line of the body (excluding head, arms and legs).

5 Spinning the service ball

The ball must be without spin or pinch during the throw up, but may, of course, have spin put on it by the bat.

6 Hitting a rising ball

Whilst serving it is a fault to hit the ball before it has started to fall.

General Faults There are several other ways to lose a point:

1 Stamping foot during service

This rather unsportsmanlike behaviour would lose you the point.

2 Touching the table

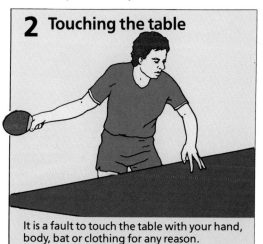

It is a fault to touch the table with your hand, body, bat or clothing for any reason.

3 Touching the net

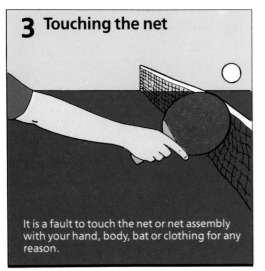

It is a fault to touch the net or net assembly with your hand, body, bat or clothing for any reason.

4 Volleying the ball

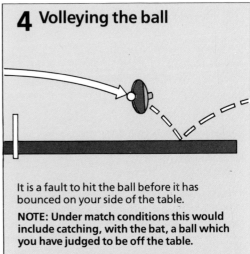

It is a fault to hit the ball before it has bounced on your side of the table.

NOTE: Under match conditions this would include catching, with the bat, a ball which you have judged to be off the table.

5 Obstructing the ball

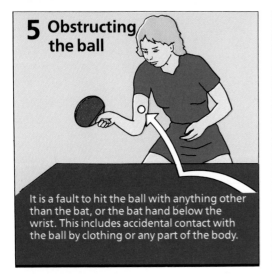

It is a fault to hit the ball with anything other than the bat, or the bat hand below the wrist. This includes accidental contact with the ball by clothing or any part of the body.

6 Playing out of doubles sequence

It is a fault to return the ball out of the correct sequence in doubles. Serving out of sequence, or playing from the wrong end, however, are not penalised. (See Non-Faults, Nos. 4 and 5.)

7 Thirteen expedite returns

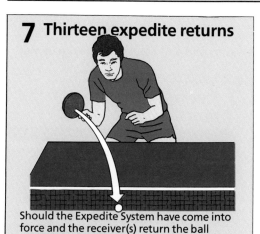

Should the Expedite System have come into force and the receiver(s) return the ball thirteen times without error, the server loses the point.

8 Hitting overhead obstructions

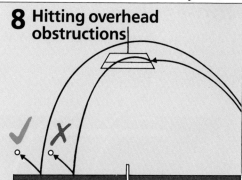

The ball may be hit as high as you wish and may pass over lights and roof beams etc., but if it hits anything other than the net assembly or the opponent's half of the table it is a fault.

9 Ball between net and post

Although the ball may legally travel round or under the net supports it may not squeeze between the edge of the net and the net support.

10 Double hit

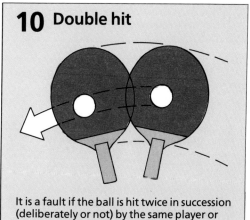

It is a fault if the ball is hit twice in succession (deliberately or not) by the same player or successively by partners in doubles.

Non-Faults

As in all games, the rules concerning genuine oversights and odd occurrences are governed by common sense.

1 Hitting the net assembly with the ball

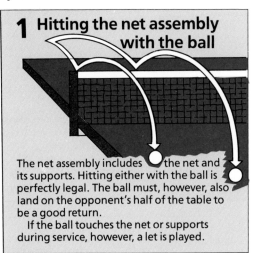

The net assembly includes the net and its supports. Hitting either with the ball is perfectly legal. The ball must, however, also land on the opponent's half of the table to be a good return.

If the ball touches the net or supports during service, however, a let is played.

2 Playing round or under the posts

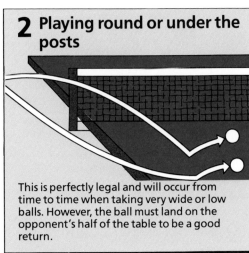

This is perfectly legal and will occur from time to time when taking very wide or low balls. However, the ball must land on the opponent's half of the table to be a good return.

3 Playing at the wrong end

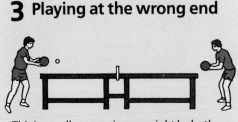

This is usually a genuine oversight by both players or pairs. Once discovered the score to date stands but the game recommences with the correct server at the correct end according to the score reached.

4 Serving out of sequence

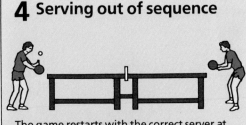

The game restarts with the correct server at the correct end according to the score at the time, which stands.

5 Serving before the opponent is ready

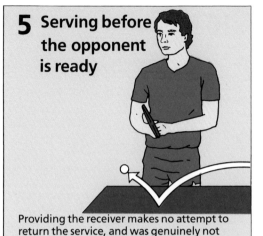

Providing the receiver makes no attempt to return the service, and was genuinely not ready, a let is played.

6 Spinning back

If the ball has bounced on your side of the table but the spin carries it back over the net, you may strike the ball while it is over your opponent's side of the table.

In fact, failure to hit the ball would lose you the point. Be careful, however, not to touch the table or net.

7 Bounce on the edge

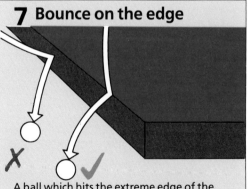

A ball which hits the extreme edge of the top of the table and flies off is a valid return.

If a ball hits the actual side of the table, however, it is a fault.

8 Playing below the table

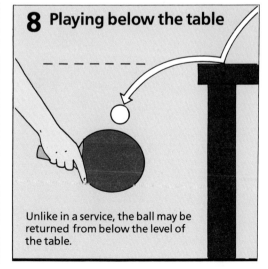

Unlike in a service, the ball may be returned from below the level of the table.

9 Bad bounce

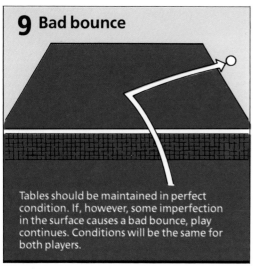

Tables should be maintained in perfect condition. If, however, some imperfection in the surface causes a bad bounce, play continues. Conditions will be the same for both players.

10 Ball break

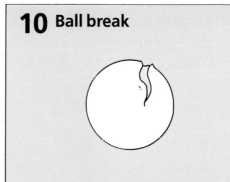

If a ball is found to have broken during a rally, play a let. However, should a point finish without a let being called, the point stands.

11 Interruption to play

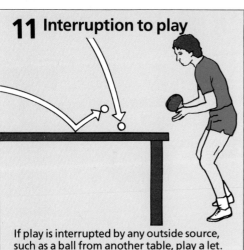

If play is interrupted by any outside source, such as a ball from another table, play a let.

12 Equipment failure

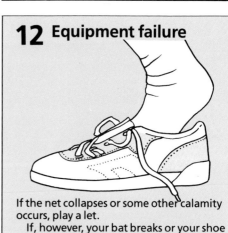

If the net collapses or some other calamity occurs, play a let.

If, however, your bat breaks or your shoe comes off it is your responsibility and you must play on and suffer the consequences.

The Grip

Grip is entirely a matter of choice, and the beginner need not worry about it unduly as the most appropriate grip will be discovered by experimentation.

There are two basic types (and many variations): the forehand tennis grip in which you shake hands with the bat, and the pen grip favoured by most Asian players.

The grip will influence your whole stroke, and the most important things to remember are:

1 The first finger and thumb control the bat. The other three fingers come into play for power shots.

2 The shoulder of the bat should be in contact with the 'V' between the thumb and forefinger.

3 Don't grip the bat too hard. Use a gentle grip for touch strokes, a firm grip for power shots.

4 Use the same grip for forehand and backhand.

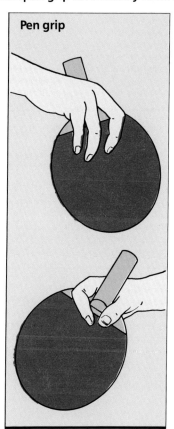

Pen grip

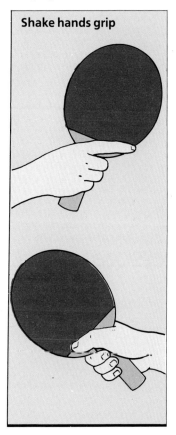

Shake hands grip

Spin

**Spin is a very significant aspect of table tennis − both for knowing how to put spin on the
ball, and for being able to counter the spin put on by an opponent.(See Returning with Spin,**

Topspin

In topspin the bat is angled forward (or closed, as
it is sometimes called), and is played with an
upward motion over the ball. As a result the ball
spins in the direction of the stroke, and shoots
forward after the bounce. The height of bounce
depends on where the bat makes contact with the
ball.

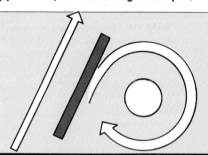

Backspin

In backspin the bat is angled backwards (open)
and played or 'chopped' in a downward motion
under the ball. As a result the ball spins in the
opposite direction to the stroke, loses speed in
flight and travels more slowly after the bounce.
The height of bounce depends on where the bat
makes contact with the ball.

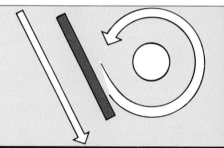

Side-spin

Side-spin is rarely used on its own. It is used in combination with either topspin or backspin.
    Instead of playing the spin straight on to the ball it is played slightly to one side or the other.
    Side-spin does not affect the speed or bounce of the ball but causes the ball to veer left or
right.
    In combination with topspin the ball will veer in the direction played; with backspin the veer
will be opposite to the direction played.

page 31.) The power in your stroke can be converted to speed, or spin, or a mixture of both. The less contact with the ball the more spin and so reversed rubber bats are better for spin as they present less friction.

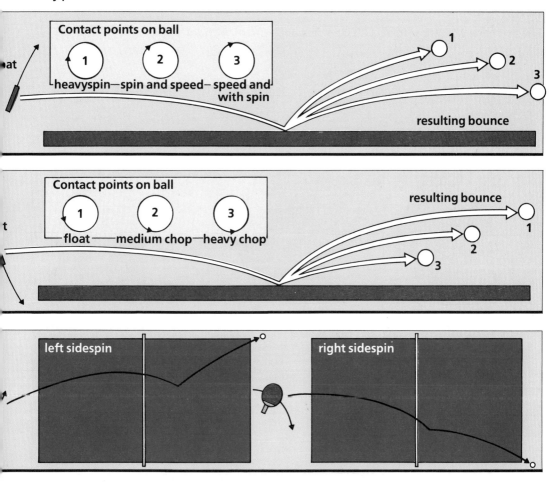

Contact points on ball

1 — heavyspin — 2 — spin and speed — 3 — speed and with spin

resulting bounce

Contact points on ball

1 — float — 2 — medium chop — 3 — heavy chop

resulting bounce

left sidespin

right sidespin

Serving

The service is the first stroke of the rally. You should try to gain the initiative. Consider your opponent's positioning and grip. Learn to serve to and from any position on the table.

Forehand

Serves can be with topspin or with backspin and with or without sidespin.

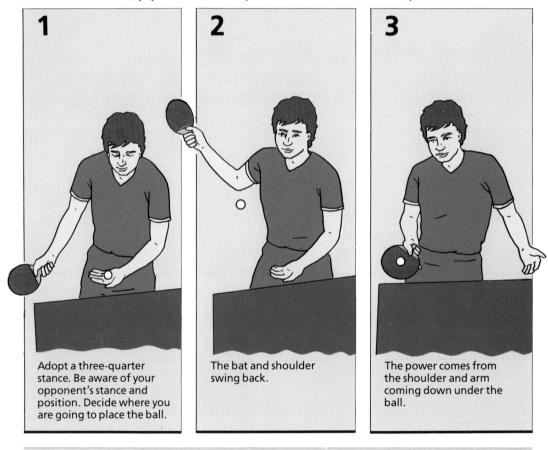

1 Adopt a three-quarter stance. Be aware of your opponent's stance and position. Decide where you are going to place the ball.

2 The bat and shoulder swing back.

3 The power comes from the shoulder and arm coming down under the ball.

Backhand

Serves can be with topspin or with backspin and with or without sidespin.

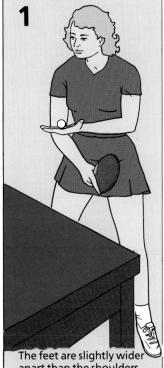

1 The feet are slightly wider apart than the shoulders. Adopt a three-quarter stance.

2 Only a short throw-up. The waist and arm put the power into the shot.

3 The ball is hit about 16-22cm above the table. Follow through afterwards and regain a steady stance for the return.

Serving Techniques

Serves can be performed with topspin, backspin, or combined with side-spin.

To begin with the serve will require practice. Start close to the net and work back until you can hit the ball from a legal position – behind the baseline.

The throw-up

Length

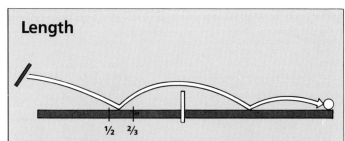

½   ⅔

A serve should be placed so that if the ball were to bounce twice on the opponent's side of the table, the second bounce would be on the baseline. This limits the receiver's options because the ball has to be played over the table.

To achieve this the ball should bounce on your side of the table half to two-thirds of the way to the net.

Wrist

Wrist action can be a powerful weapon. Try to relax the grip and keep the wrist loose.

More advanced players use wrist action to impart spin.

A ball hit in position A has the opposite spin to a ball hit in position B.

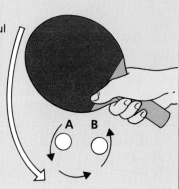

The ball is thrown up with the free hand. High throws can yield more potential spin because the ball is falling faster when the bat hits it.

But high throw-ups require perfect co-ordination and are not for the beginner.

Height of ball

Whether playing topspin or backspin you should try to hit the ball always at the right height. Beginners always find they have to hit the ball quite high but a good player would expect to hit the ball as low as possible – about 15-22 cm above the table.

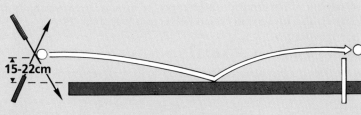

15-22cm

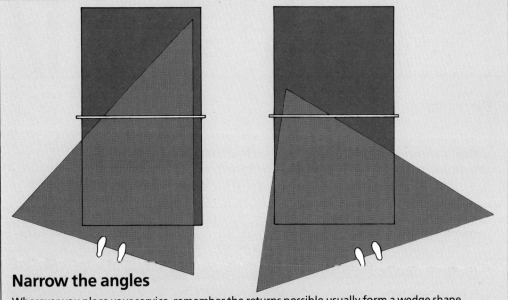

Narrow the angles

Wherever you place your service, remember the returns possible usually form a wedge shape.
   After the service, position yourself in the middle of the back of the wedge so you are ready for any return.

Receiving Service

When receiving service it is essential to read the spin. This means watching for the upward movement of the bat for topspin and the downward movement of the bat for backspin.

Watch also for the deceptive wrist spins (see page 28).

A Block or Push

A block or push return is the most basic form of return. It effectively neutralises the server's spin putting little or no spin on your return.

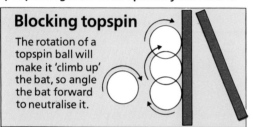

Blocking topspin

The rotation of a topspin ball will make it 'climb up' the bat, so angle the bat forward to neutralise it.

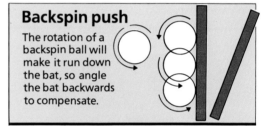

Backspin push

The rotation of a backspin ball will make it run down the bat, so angle the bat backwards to compensate.

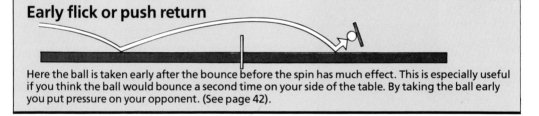

Early flick or push return

Here the ball is taken early after the bounce before the spin has much effect. This is especially useful if you think the ball would bounce a second time on your side of the table. By taking the ball early you put pressure on your opponent. (See page 42).

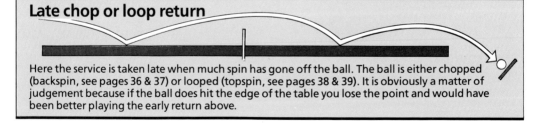

Late chop or loop return

Here the service is taken late when much spin has gone off the ball. The ball is either chopped (backspin, see pages 36 & 37) or looped (topspin, see pages 38 & 39). It is obviously a matter of judgement because if the ball does hit the edge of the table you lose the point and would have been better playing the early return above.

Returning with Spin

It is possible to return with spin. The easiest return is that which keeps the spin in the same direction.

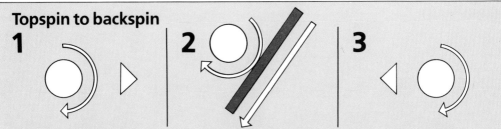

Topspin to backspin

1 **2** **3**

A topspin service tumbles forwards, so if you chop downwards you are playing in the same direction as the spin.

Once you hit the ball, however, because it is moving in the opposite direction it becomes a backspin return.

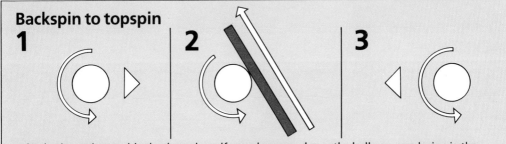

Backspin to topspin

1 **2** **3**

A backspin service tumbles backwards, so if you play up and over the ball you are playing in the same direction as the spin.

Once you hit the ball, however, it becomes a topspin return.

Side-spin can be dealt with in the same way, but remember to play 'outside' the ball because it will move away from you.

Many players also reverse the spin, returning a topspin with a topspin etc.

To do this the bat must 'stroke' the ball in the opposite direction to the spin. To be effective the bat's speed must be greater than that of the spin on the ball, and the angle of the bat set to neutralise the spin as if playing a block or push.

Block Shot

This is a simple shot used against topspin. The bat is always played closed or forward to neutralise the opponent's spin.

FOREHAND

BACKHAND

Push Shot

This equally simple shot is used against slower shots or backspin shots. The bat is always played open or backwards. Depending on your stroke it may impart some backspin.

FOREHAND

BACKHAND

The Topspin Drive

This is the classic attacking stroke in table tennis. The power comes from a combination of footwork and body action. The action is upwards to impart topspin.

FOREHAND

1

Stand off square, with the knees slightly bent and the elbow at 90°.

2

Three-quarters of the swing is before the shot, one-quarter to one-third afterwards.

Hit the ball at the top of its bounce.

The shoulders rotate a quarter turn. The power comes from turning back into the ball.

3

Accelerate the arm onto and over the ball. Follow through until the bat is pointing after the ball.

BACKHAND

1

The stroke is played square or slightly off square. Take the ball in front of the body.
There is much less swing than in the forehand.

2

The power comes from the forearm and wrist.

3

Final speed can be added by flicking the wrist at the last moment.
Follow through until the bat points after the ball.

Bounce

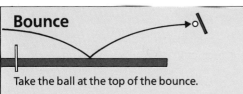

Take the ball at the top of the bounce.

Angle

If you return diagonally, you have more room for your shot and are less likely to miss the table.

The Chop Shot

This is the classic defensive stroke. The player retreats a little from the table to deal with a really fierce attacking shot. The action is downwards to impart backspin.

FOREHAND

1

The bat starts at head height and descends in line with the ball.
   Very little forward motion is needed as the force of your opponent's shot can be rebounded.

2

Take the ball as late as possible: you will lose speed but gain control.

3

Follow through down and forward until the arm is straight.

BACKHAND

1

Take the shoulder and leg back in line with the ball. Raise the bat to head height.

2

Chop down taking the ball as late as possible using its own momentum and a small push forward.

3

Follow through – down and forward until the arm is straight.

Loop Shots

These are exaggerated topspin drives. Whereas the drive emphasises speed, the loop emphasises spin.

FOREHAND

1

Get down to an almost sitting position, and use the legs to drive upwards.
   The major part of the swing is *before* the shot.

2

Use the waist to twist into the shot for added power, taking the ball at the top of the bounce or just after.

3

Follow through in the direction of the ball and into the ready position for the next stroke.

BACKHAND

The backhand loop is not as easy or effective as the forehand loop. Fast players often prefer to run round the shot and take it on the forehand.

1

The stance is square to the table.

2

Using the wrist and arm, the bat accelerates upwards through nearly 180°.

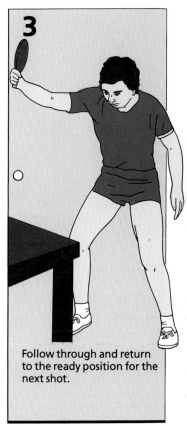

3

Follow through and return to the ready position for the next shot.

The Lob

A strictly defensive shot used against a smash or very fast topspin drive, the lob can be played forehand or backhand.

It is a topspin drive or loop deliberately played as high as possible to gain extra time.

Put as much topspin on the ball as possible to ensure the ball shoots forward after the bounce, keeping the opponent back from the table.

Use the legs, waist and a very fast arm action.

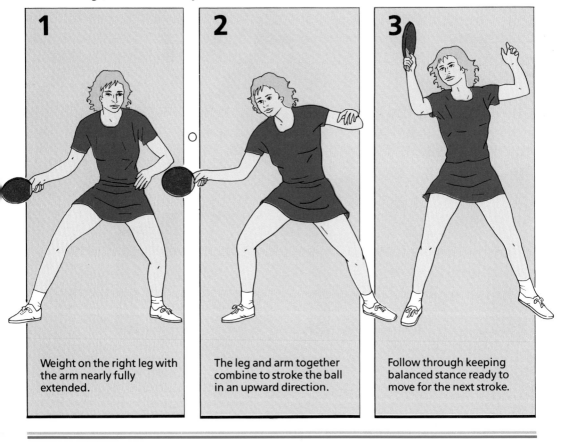

1 Weight on the right leg with the arm nearly fully extended.

2 The leg and arm together combine to stroke the ball in an upward direction.

3 Follow through keeping balanced stance ready to move for the next stroke.

The Smash

The smash is the hardest drive you can play. Spin is of less importance than power.

The whole body-weight is thrown behind the bat. The ball, which is most commonly a high return, is taken early and punished mercilessly.

Watch the angle of your bat – many smashes end up in the net or off the table owing to over – excitement and sloppy angles.

Remember – keep an open bat against backspin, and a closed one against topspin.

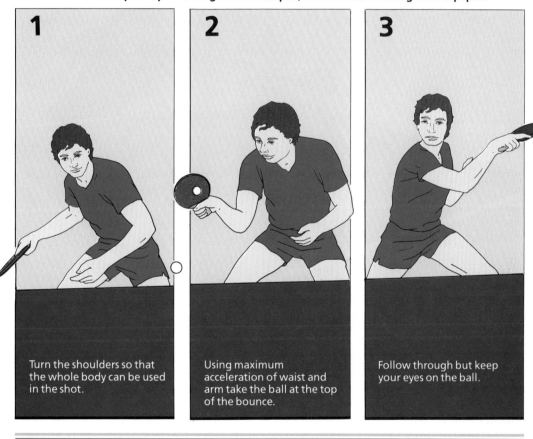

1 Turn the shoulders so that the whole body can be used in the shot.

2 Using maximum acceleration of waist and arm take the ball at the top of the bounce.

3 Follow through but keep your eyes on the ball.

The Drop Shot

This shot – sometimes disguised, sometimes not – is played when your opponent has dropped back from the table.

Take all the speed out of the ball with a relaxed wrist. Hit the ball early and, compensating for spin, let it just clear the net and drop onto your opponent's half of the table.

Do not bother with spin, concentrate on using the minimum amount of speed needed to just clear the net.

The Flick

The flick is used when returning serve and in normal play. Approach the ball as if playing a push but then at the last second turn the bat over the ball for a more aggressive shot.

Bad Habits

As mentioned in the Introduction, bad habits are hard to cure. It is easier to learn to do things right than to 'unlearn' things you are doing wrong. Here are some common bad habits found in beginners.

1 Bad grip

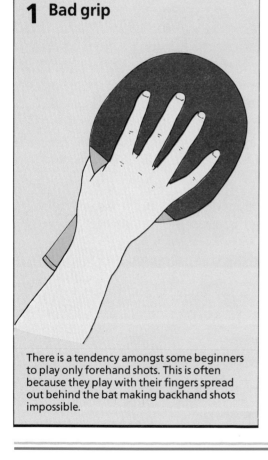

There is a tendency amongst some beginners to play only forehand shots. This is often because they play with their fingers spread out behind the bat making backhand shots impossible.

2 Standing too far from the table

You should stand about the distance of your bat and arm from the table and adopt the ready stances shown. From this position you will get the greatest accuracy since you are nearest to your target – the table.

3 Mobility and lack of recovery

After playing a shot you will be watching for its return. Whilst you MUST always watch the ball, do not stay rooted to the spot. Remember to get back to a central position in the ready stance.

4 Going for speed

It is very understandable that beginners want to improve and emulate the speed of experienced players but this is a serious mistake. It is much more important to learn control and accurate placement of your shots before attempting speed.

5 Avoiding weak shots

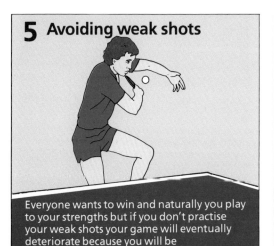

Everyone wants to win and naturally you play to your strengths but if you don't practise your weak shots your game will eventually deteriorate because you will be compensating for your weaknesses.

6 Playing with legs straight

Footwork is vital in table tennis and if you are stiff and upright you will never achieve the mobility necessary. Learn to play all the time with your knees flexed and your weight as evenly balanced as possible.

Doubles Tactics

Because returns are taken in strict rotation, doubles table tennis requires a high degree of co-operation between partners.

Service

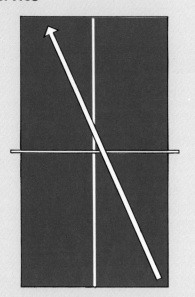

Because the serve is always from the right-hand side, it is not such an important part of the game as in singles. Both services and returns are limited. However, always remember your partner has to play the next shot so serve accordingly.

Co-ordinating with your partner

Most people can play doubles together but some combinations are naturally more successful. A right and left-handed combination is good, as is two topspin hitters. Other good partnerships are hitters and loopers, and hitters and blockers. You will note that one partner at least must be a hitter to succeed.

Getting out of your partner's way

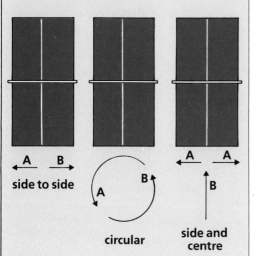

side to side

circular

side and centre

There are many ways of doing this and partners must work it out before they begin to play. If your partner serves forehand, stand on the backhand side and vice versa for a backhand serve. You can move in from side to side or front to back or even in a circular motion but the important factor is to place the ball so it comes back for your partner's strong shots and to be in a good position to come in to play yours.

Play your opponents into trouble

A good doubles partnership made up of average players should beat two good players who have never played together before. That's how important tactics are in doubles.

Players should try either to set shots up for each other – a loop player setting up high returns for a hitter, for example – or to play to confound their opponents eg. by playing to their forehands one after the other to force them both to one side of the table.

Glossary

BACKSPIN — The spin which results from a downward movement of the bat under the ball.

BLOCK — A simple shot played against topspin shots with the bat angled forward.

CHOP — A defensive shot, like an exaggerated push shot, imparting a lot of backspin.

DRIVE — A more aggressive block shot but with the emphasis on speed rather than spin.

DROP SHOT — A shot played with the minimum force to drop close to the net on the opponent's side of the table.

EXPEDITE SYSTEM — A system which is brought into play either with the consent of both players or after a game has lasted 15 minutes.

HALF VOLLEY — A shot played immediately after the ball has bounced.

LET — A rally the result of which is not scored.

LOB — A defensive shot in which the ball is returned very high with topspin to gain extra time.

LOOP — A more aggressive block shot with the emphasis on spin rather than speed.

PEN GRIP — A style of grip, made popular by oriental players, in which the bat is held a little like a pen.

PUSH — A simple shot played against slow or backspin shots with the bat angled backwards.

RALLY — The period during which the ball remains in play.

SHAKE HANDS GRIP — The most popular grip, and self-explanatory.

SMASH — A very hard drive played for speed alone.

TOPSPIN — The spin which results from an upward movement of the bat brushing the ball lightly.

VOLLEY — A shot played after the ball has crossed the net but before it has touched the table. Note: this is a fault.